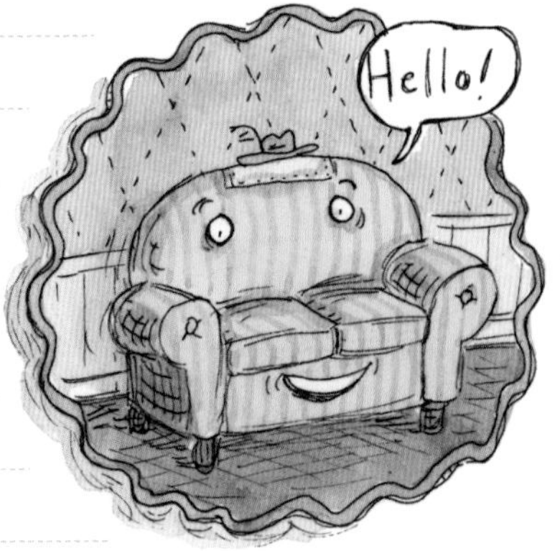
Hello!

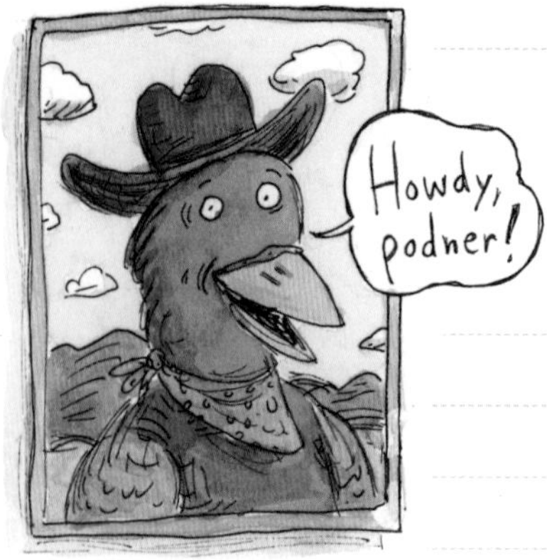
Howdy, podner!

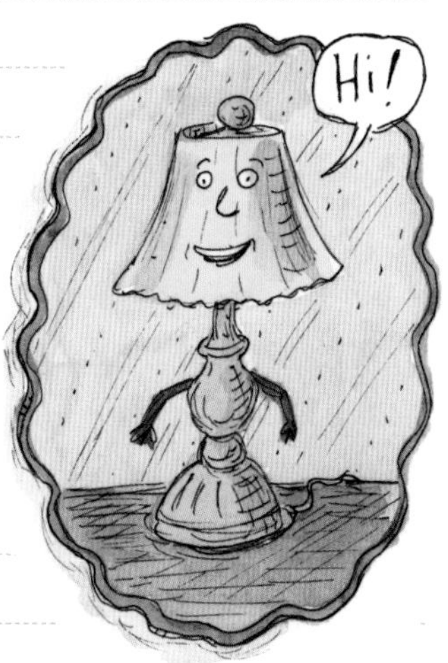
Hi!

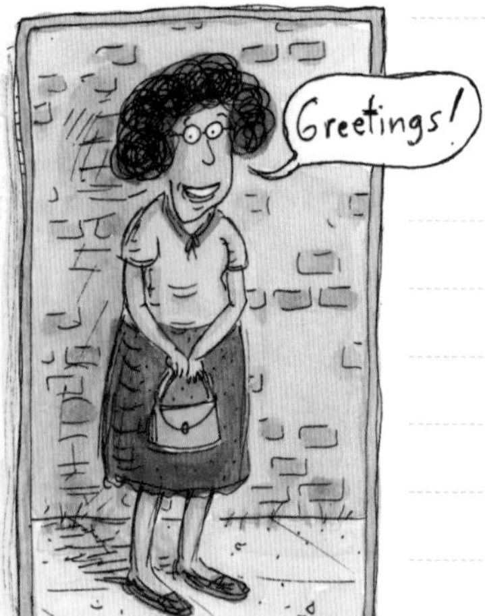
Greetings!

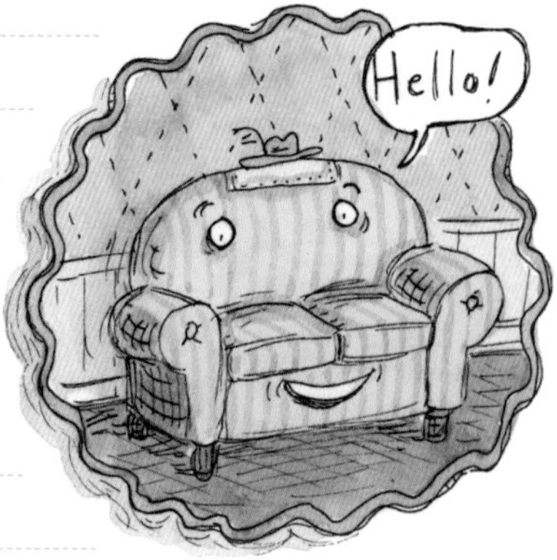
Hello!

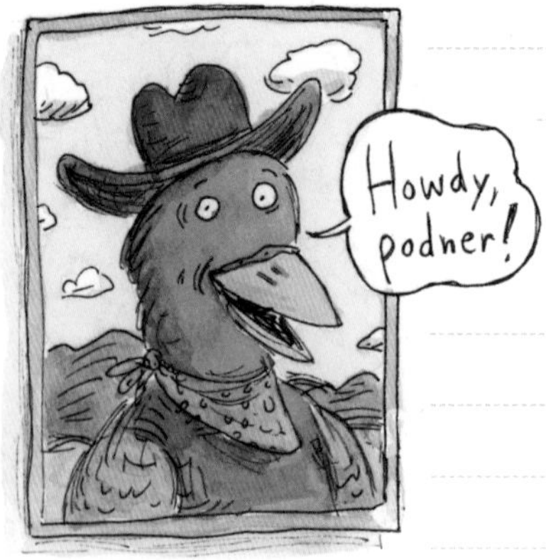
Howdy, podner!

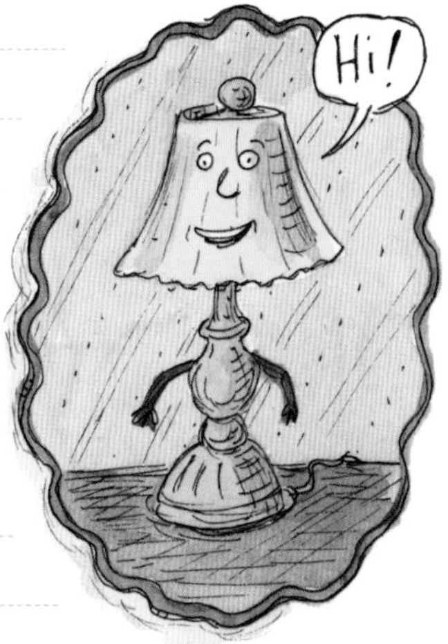
Hi!

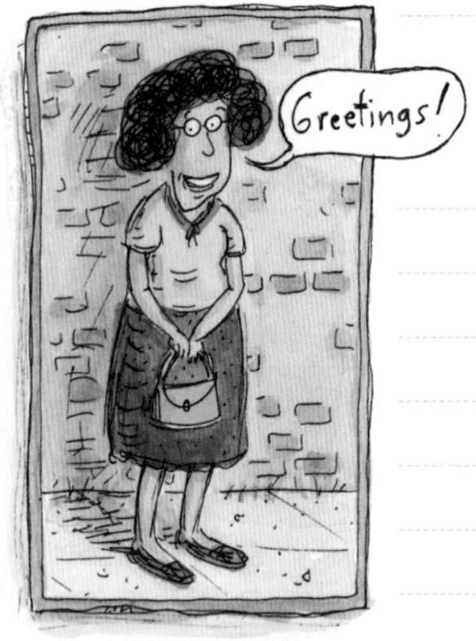
Greetings!

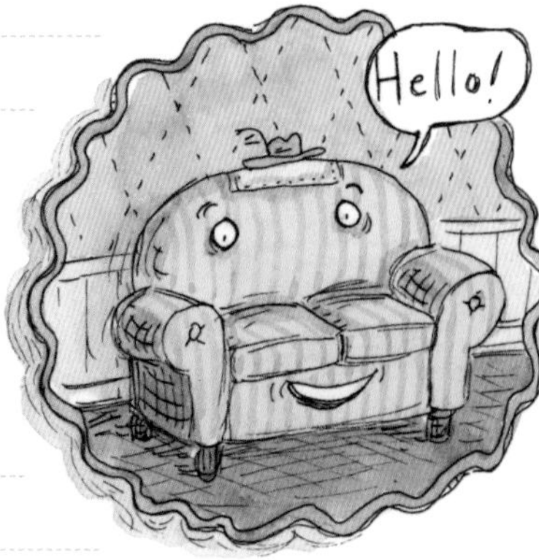
Hello!

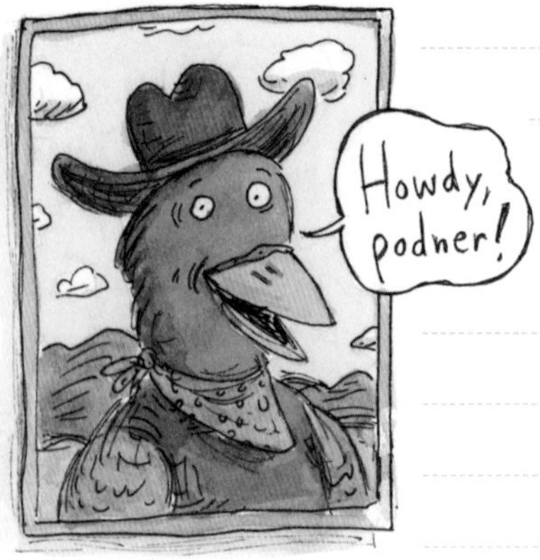
Howdy, podner!

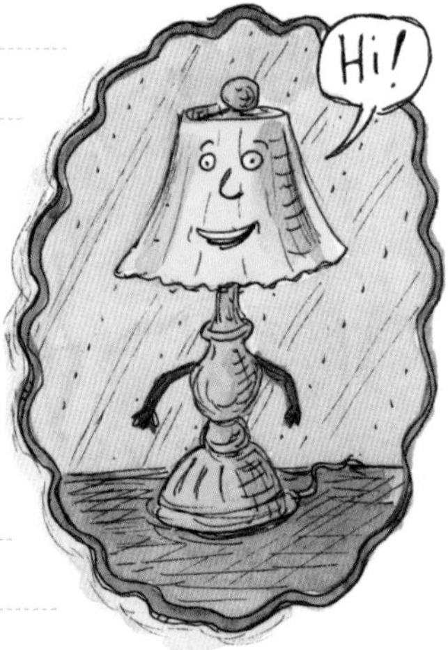
Hi!

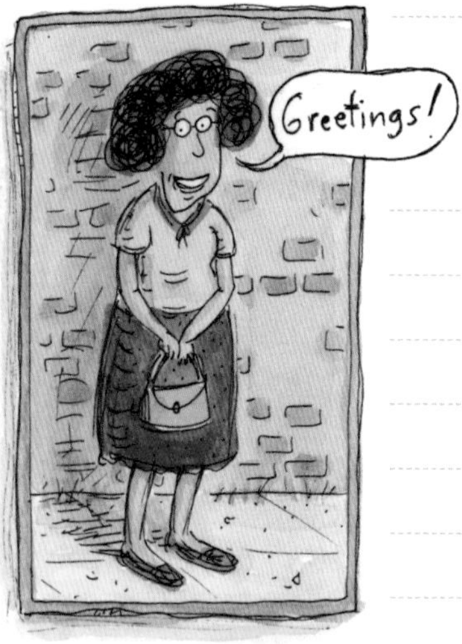
Greetings!

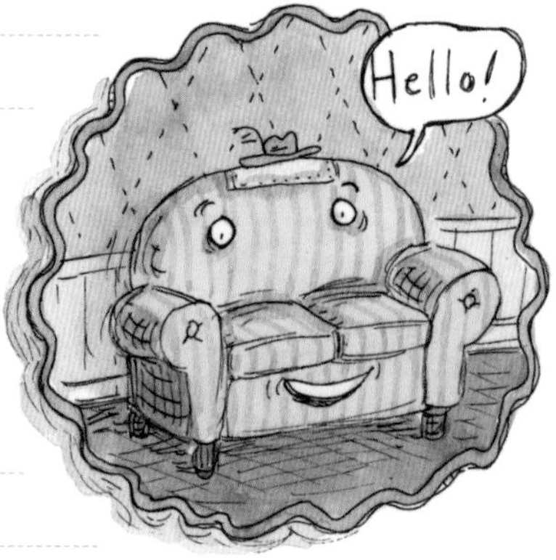
Hello!

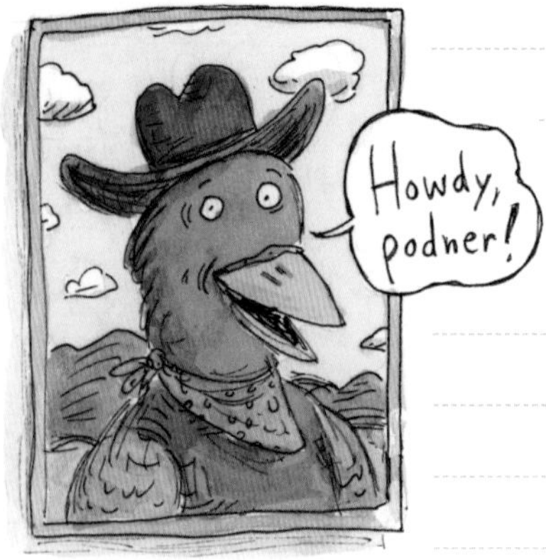
Howdy, podner!

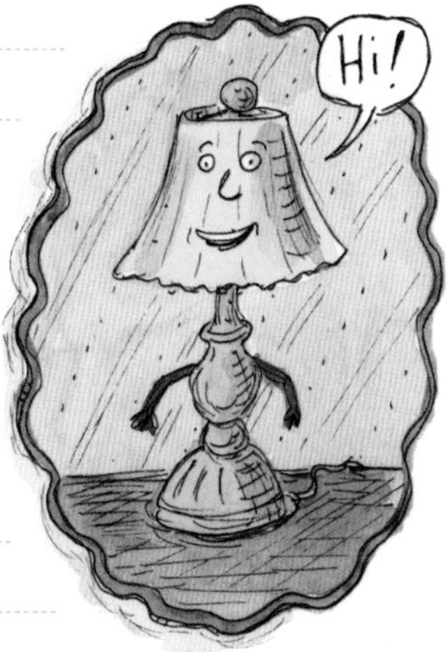
Hi!

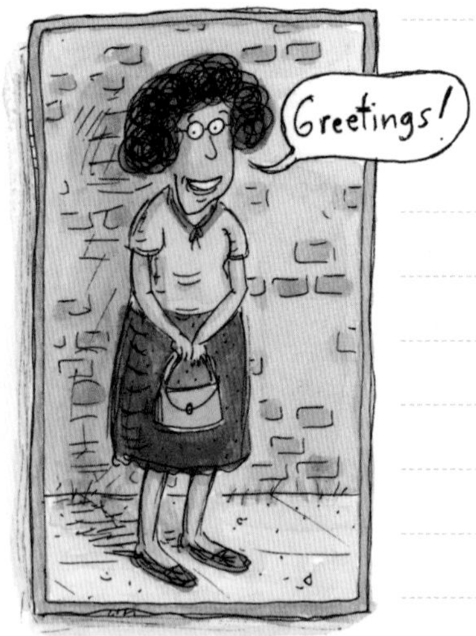
Greetings!

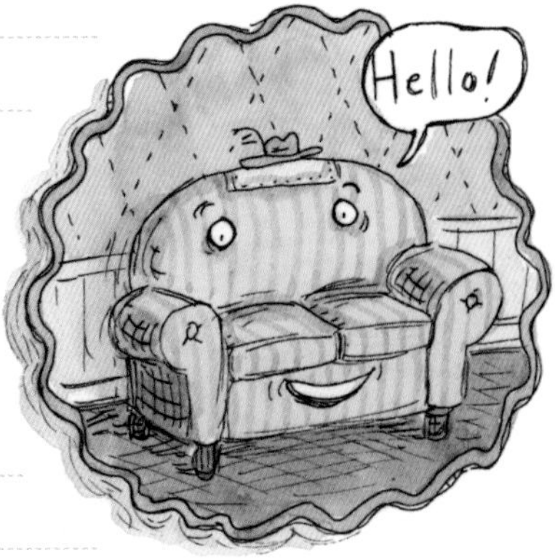
Hello!

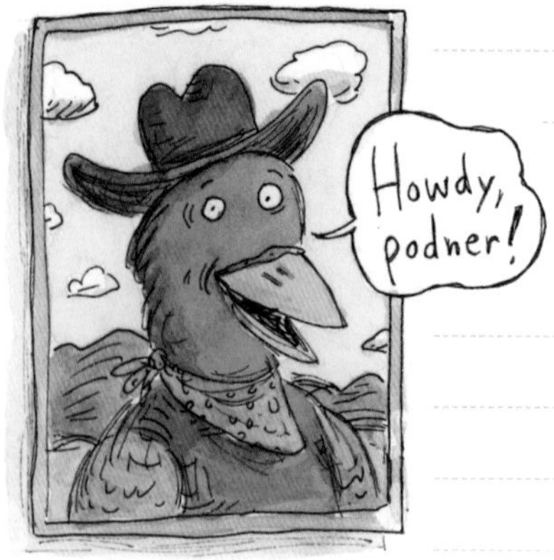
Howdy, podner!

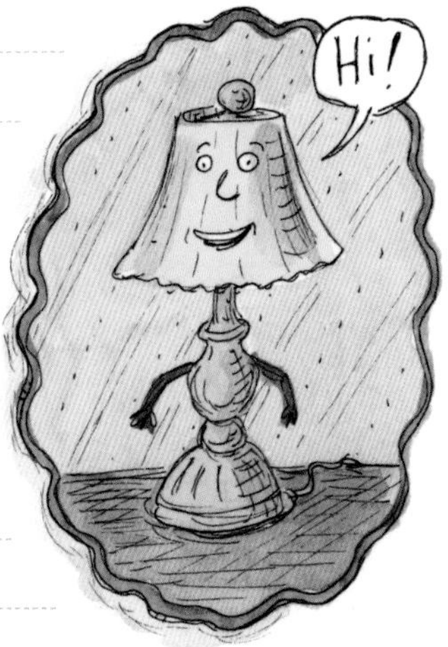
Hi!

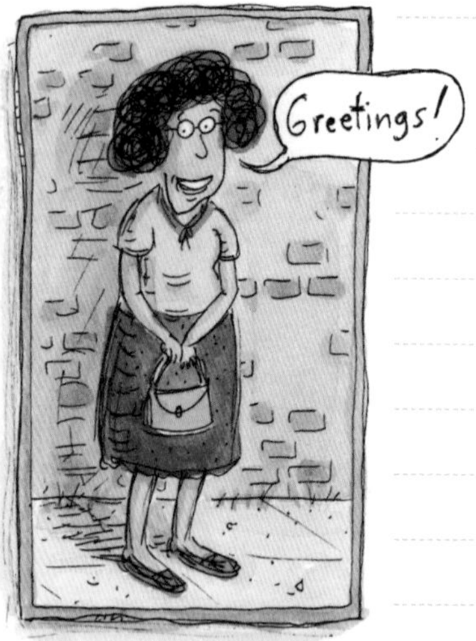
Greetings!

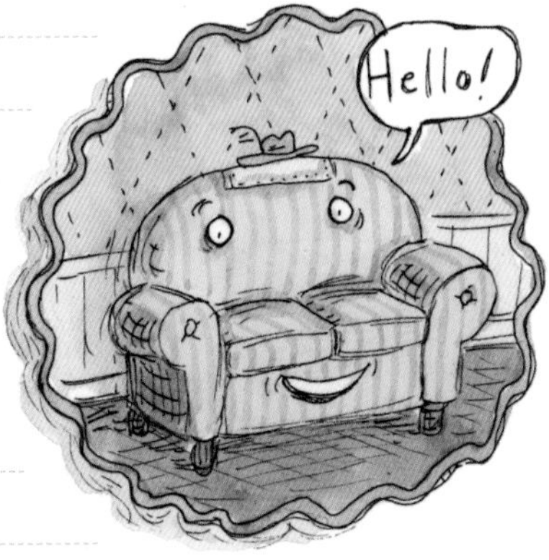
Hello!

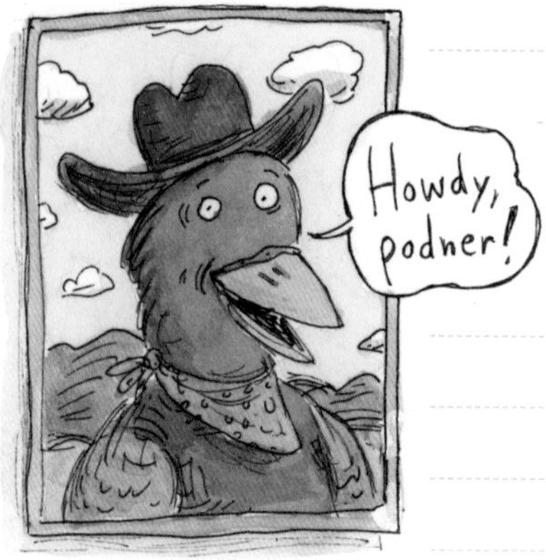
Howdy, podner!

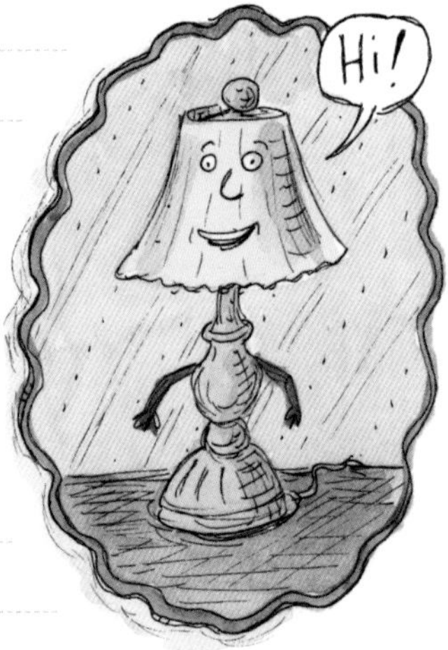
Hi!

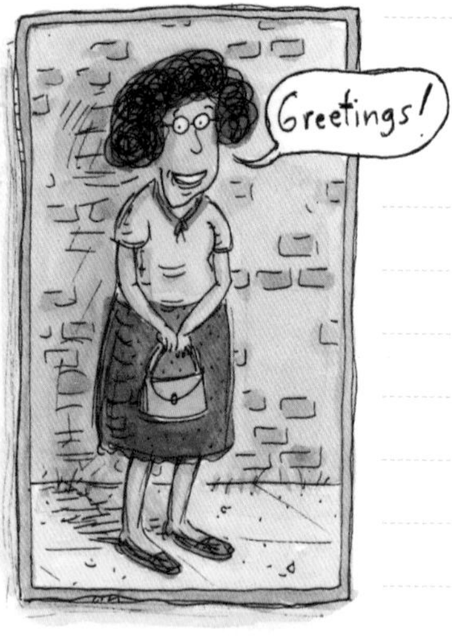
Greetings!

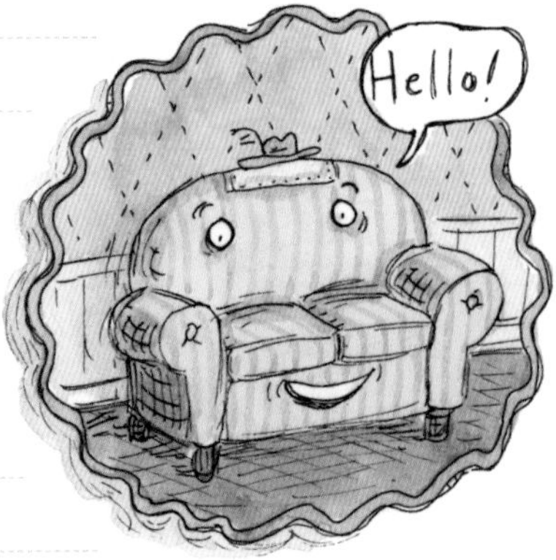
Hello!

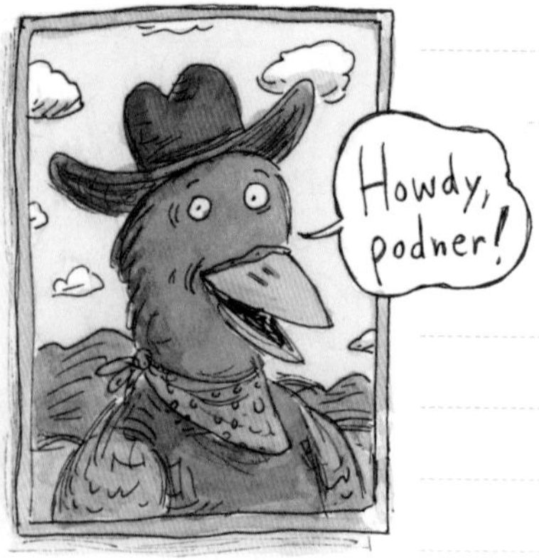
Howdy, podner!

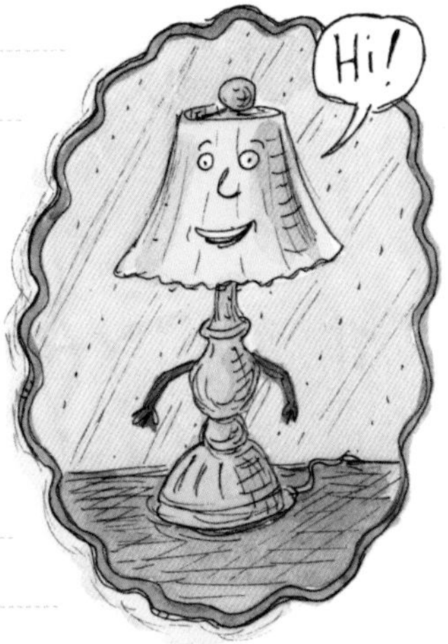
Hi!

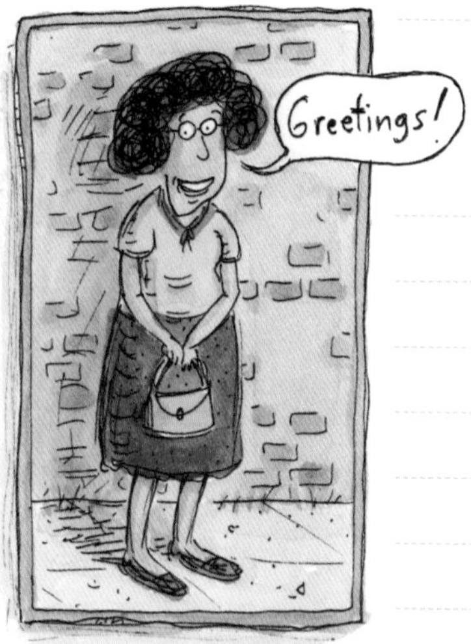
Greetings!

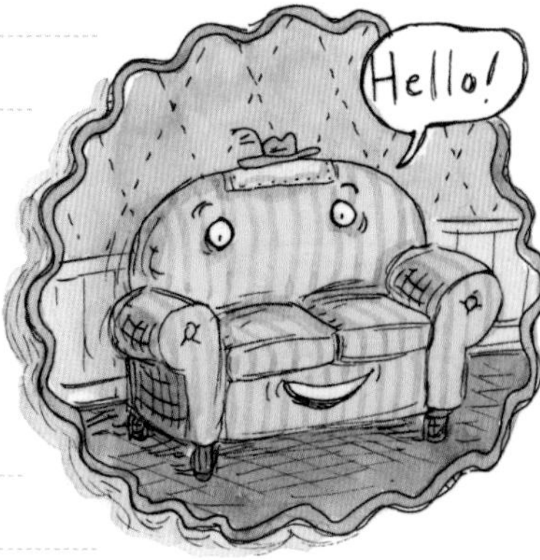
Hello!

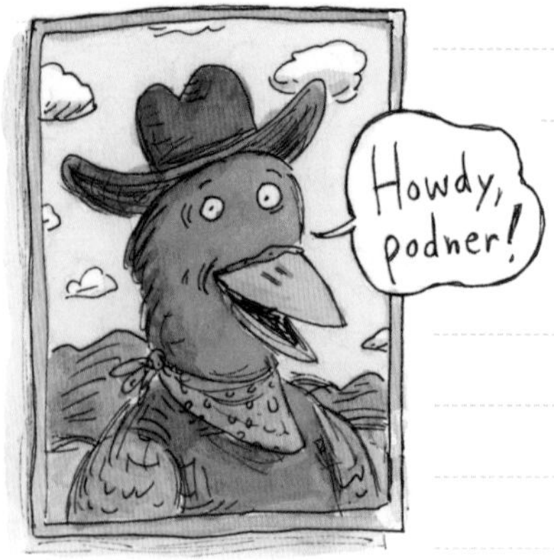
Howdy, podner!

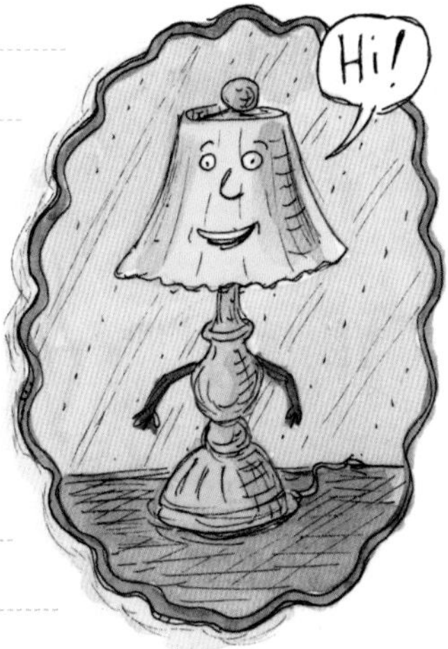
Hi!

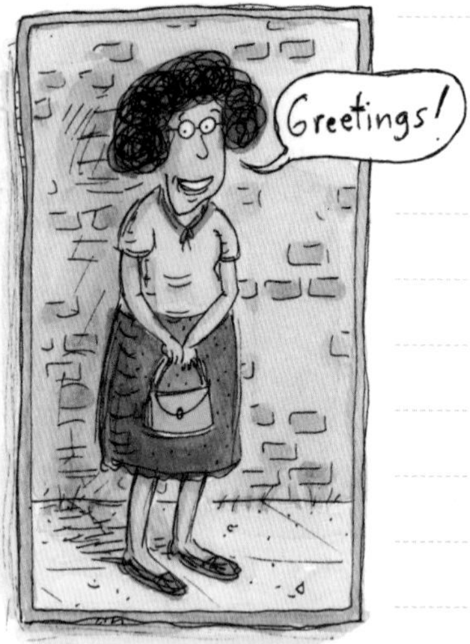
Greetings!

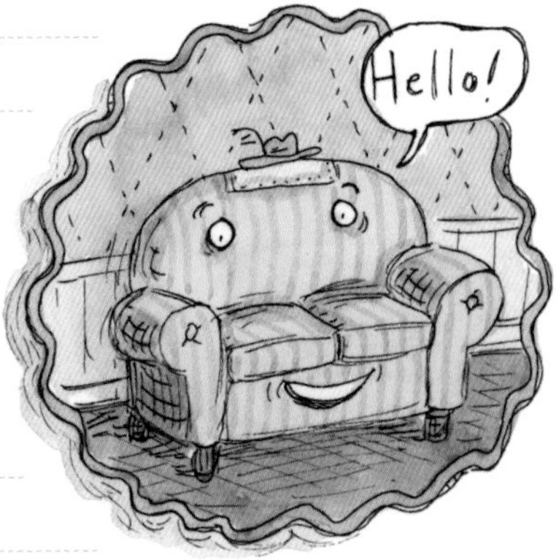
Hello!

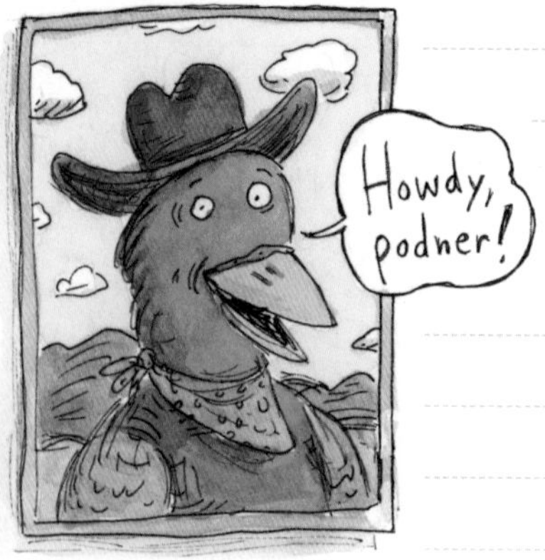
Howdy, podner!

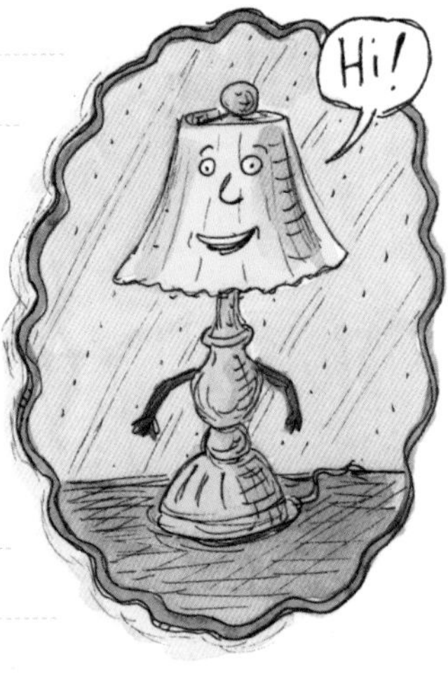
Hi!

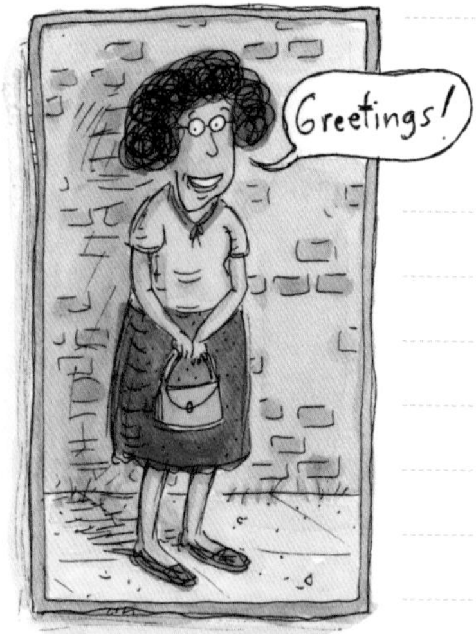
Greetings!

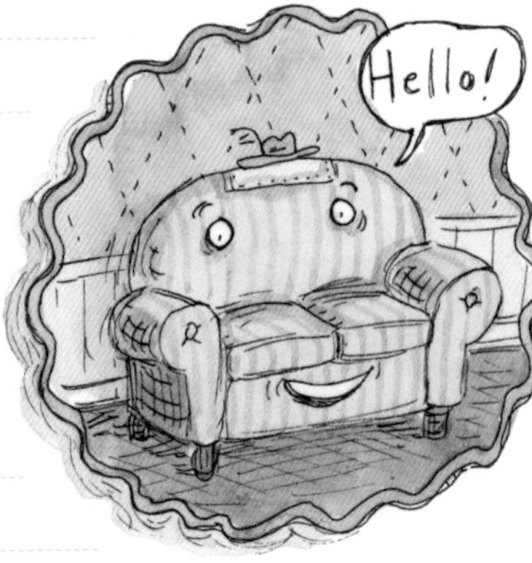
Hello!

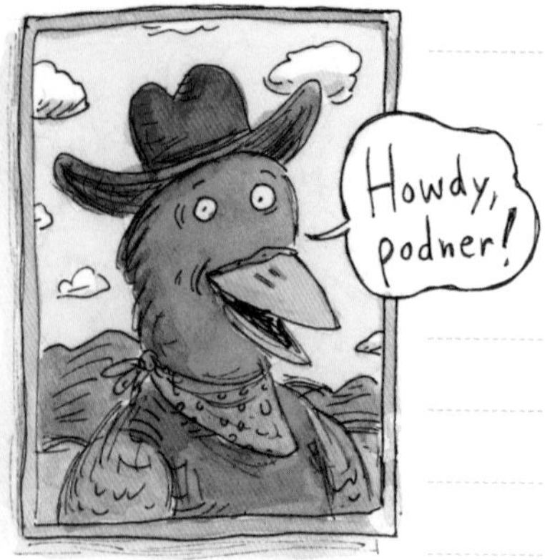
Howdy, podner!

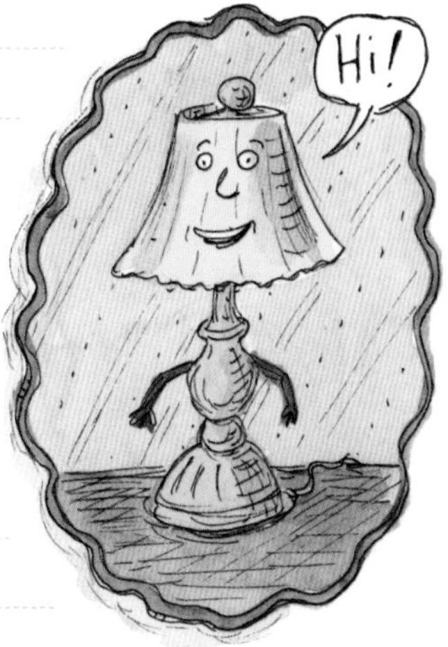
Hi!

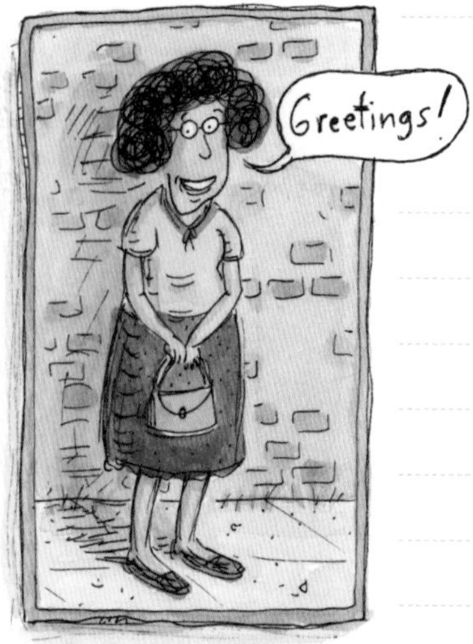
Greetings!

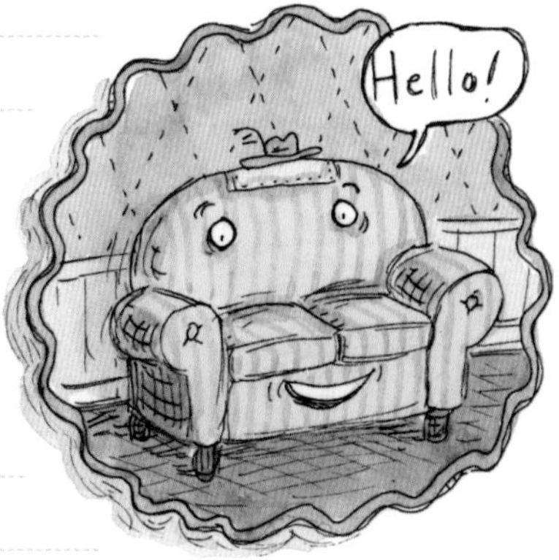
Hello!

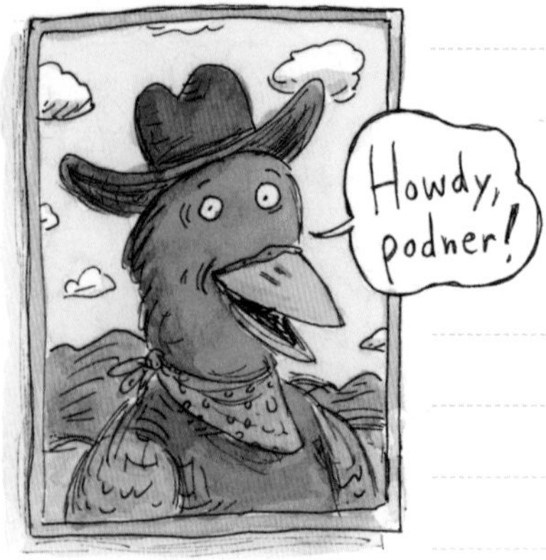
Howdy, podner!

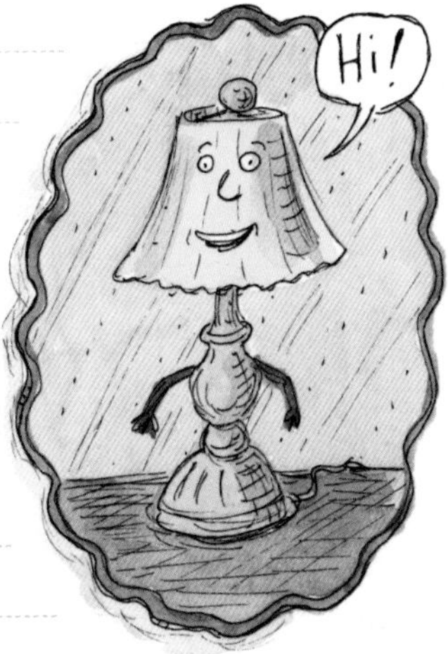
Hi!

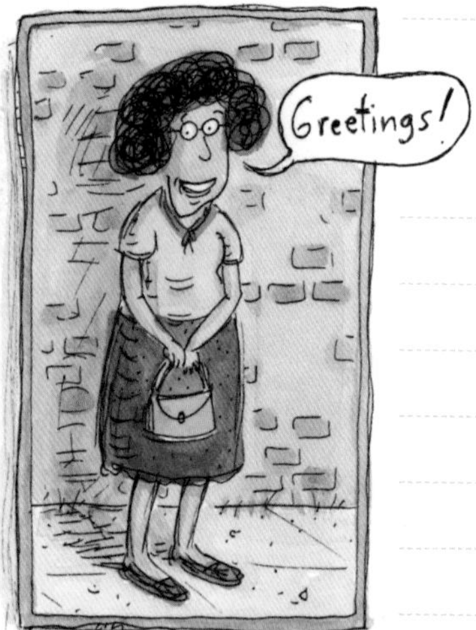
Greetings!

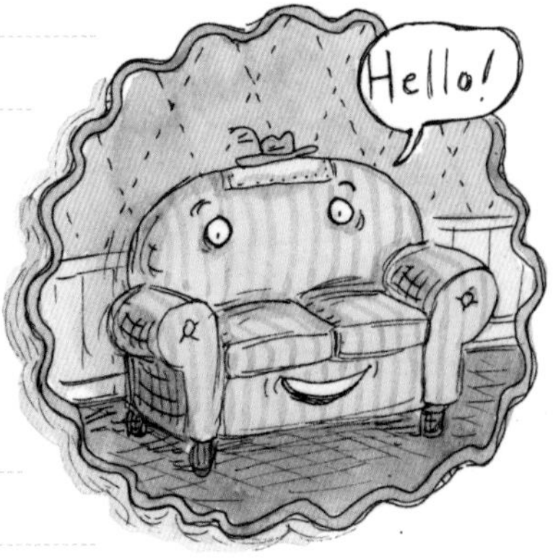
Hello!

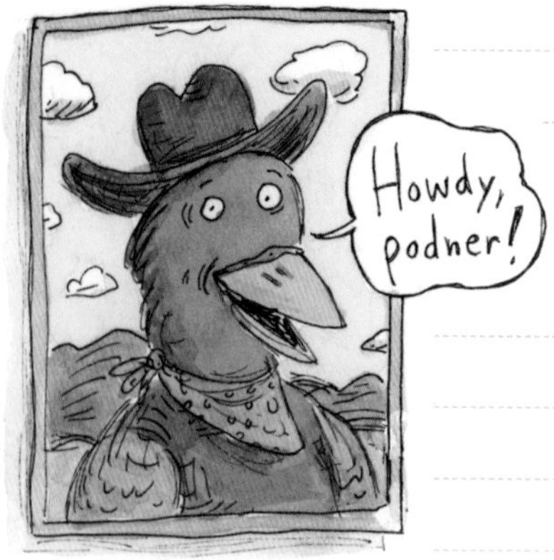
Howdy, podner!

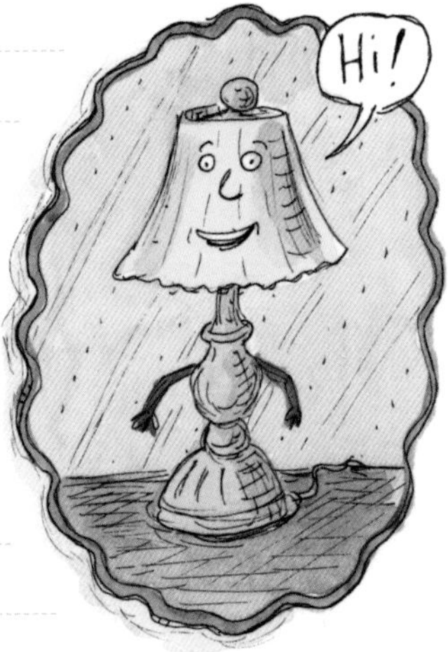
Hi!

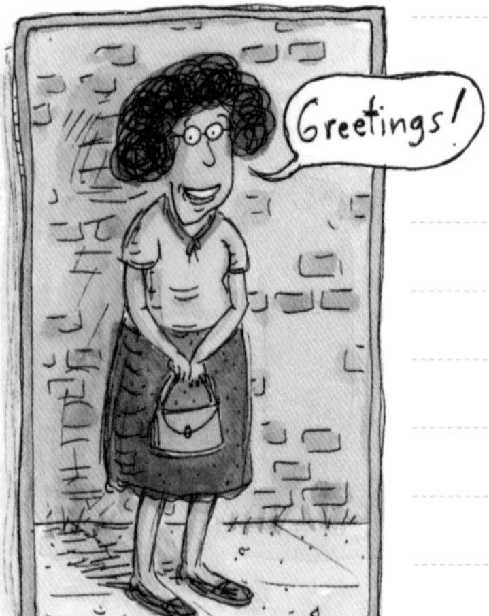
Greetings!

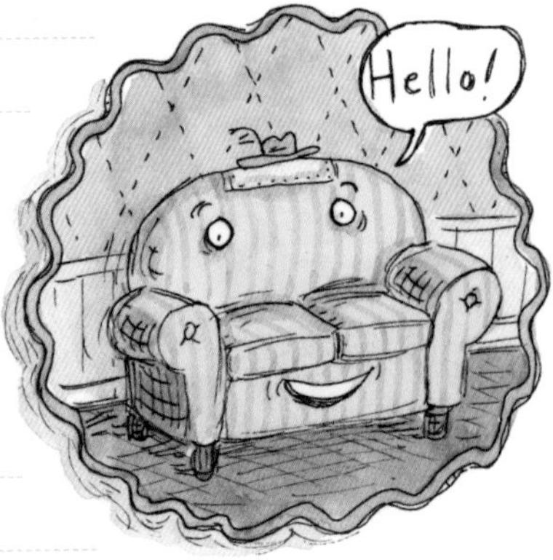
Hello!

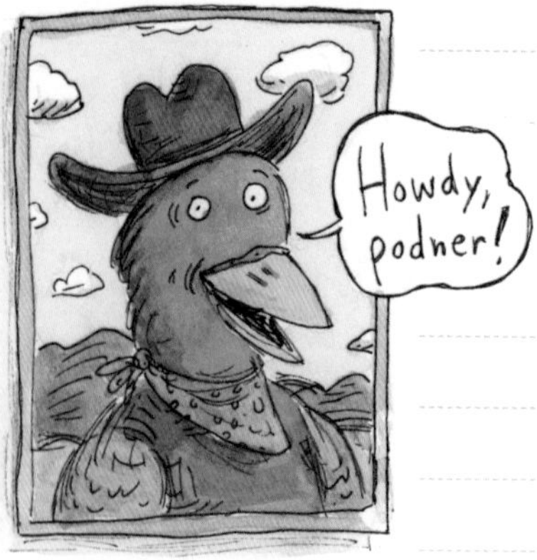
Howdy, podner!

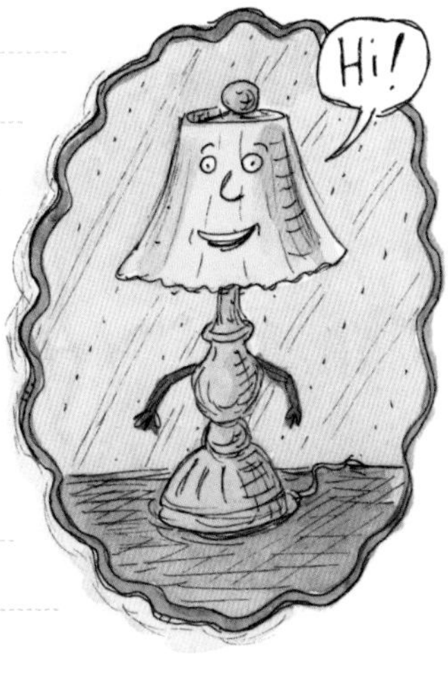
Hi!

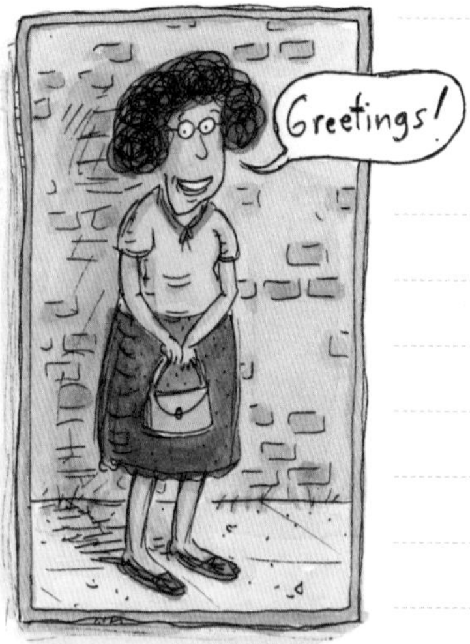
Greetings!

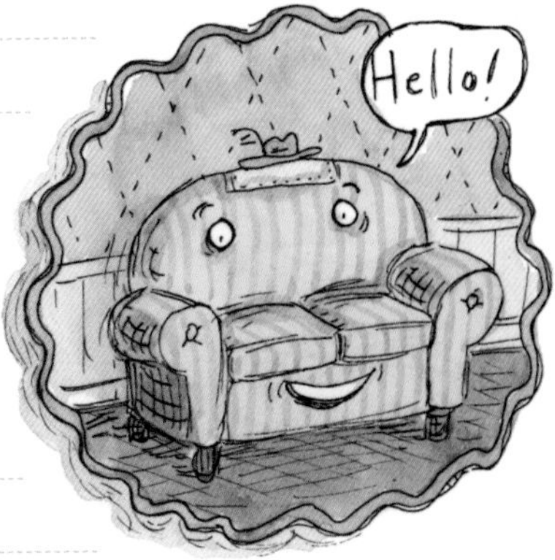
Hello!

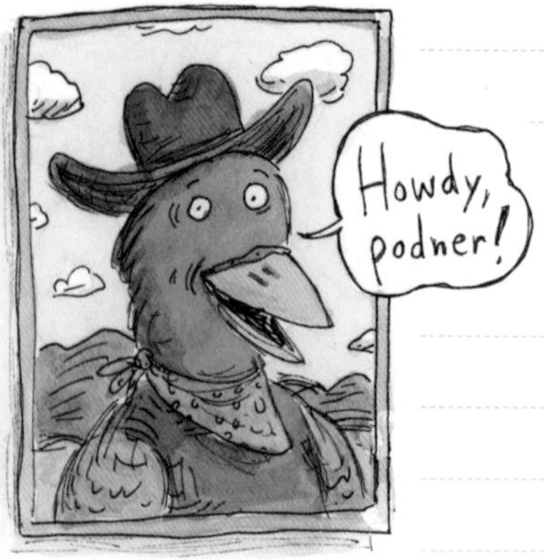
Howdy, podner!

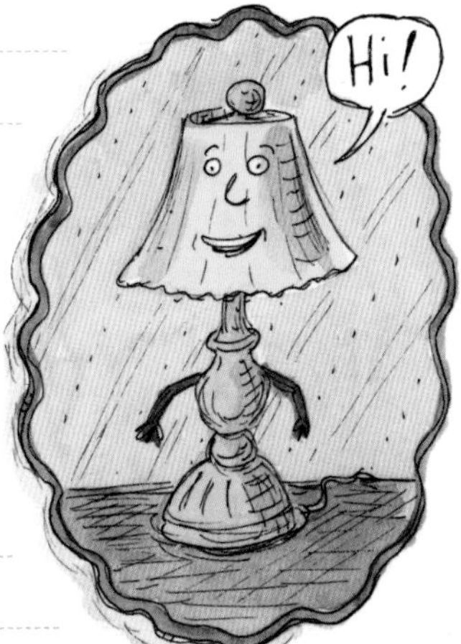
Hi!

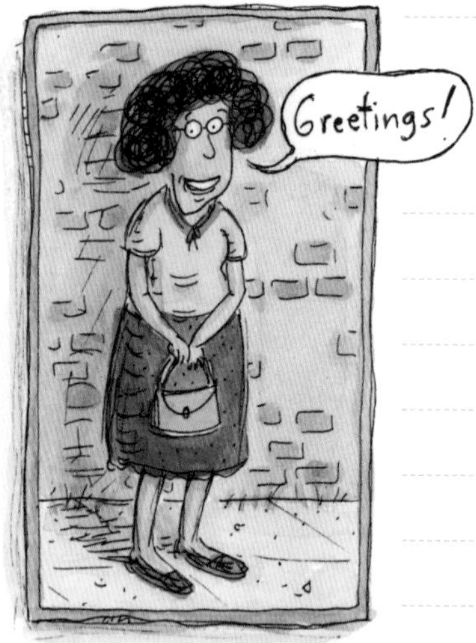
Greetings!

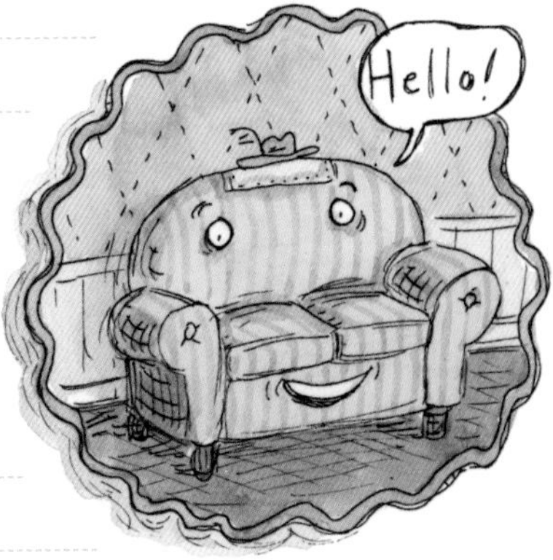
Hello!

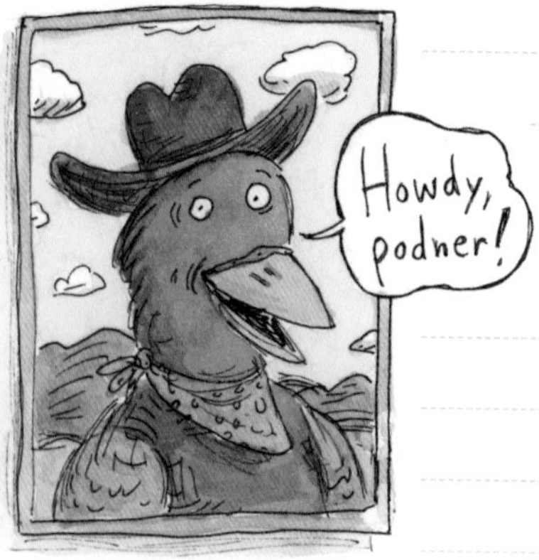
Howdy, podner!

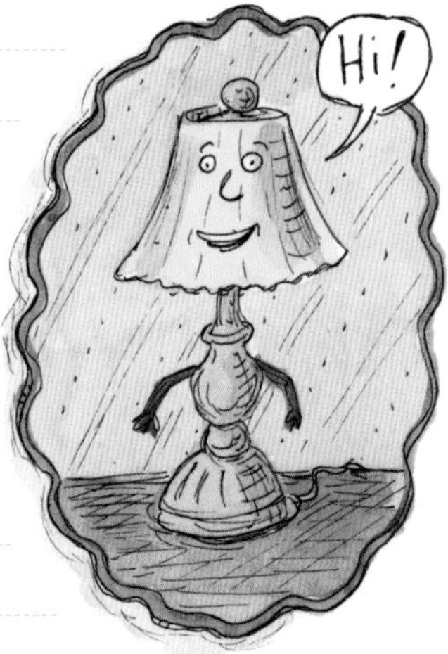
Hi!

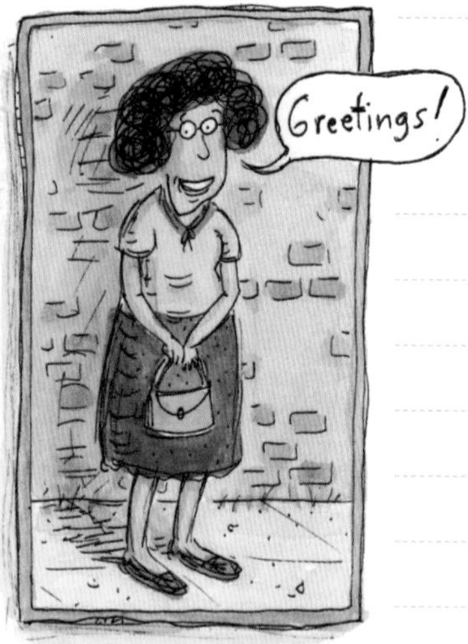
Greetings!

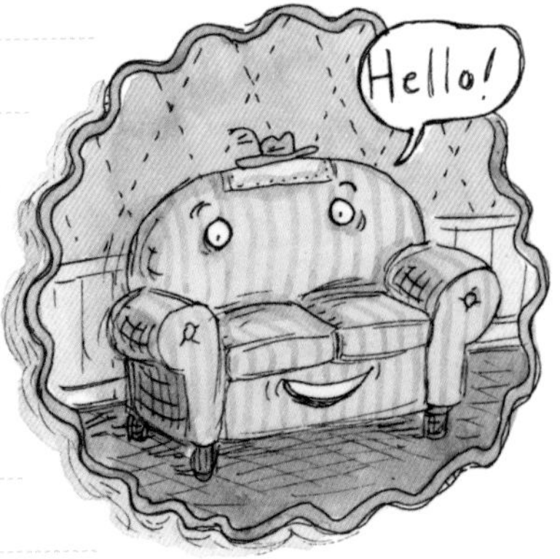
Hello!

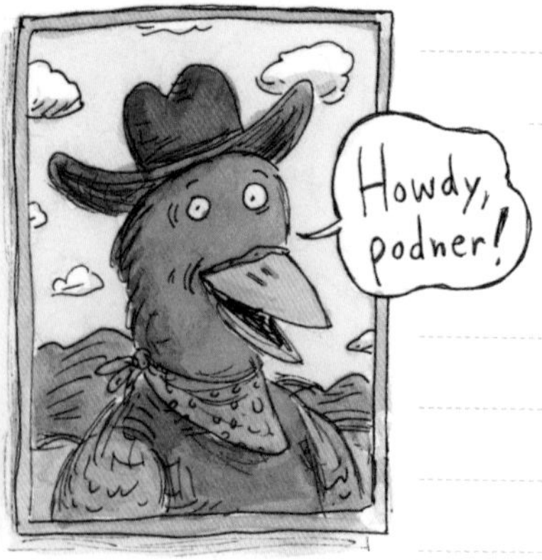
Howdy, podner!

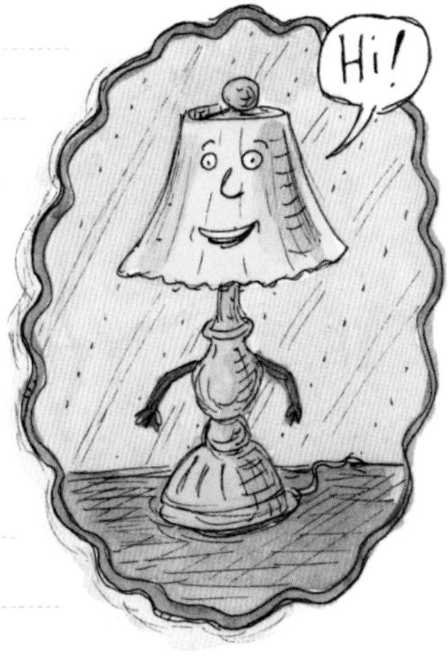
Hi!

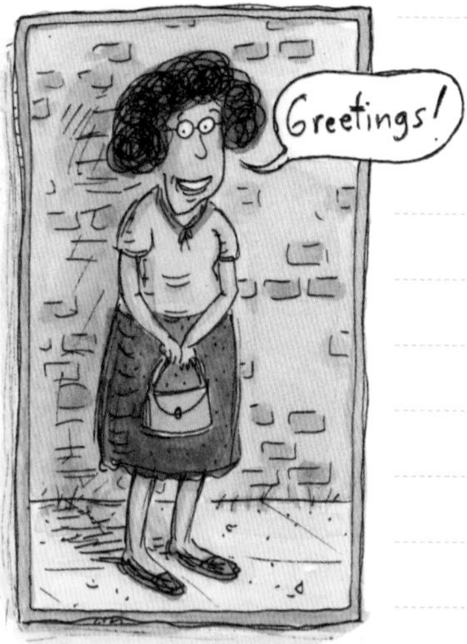
Greetings!

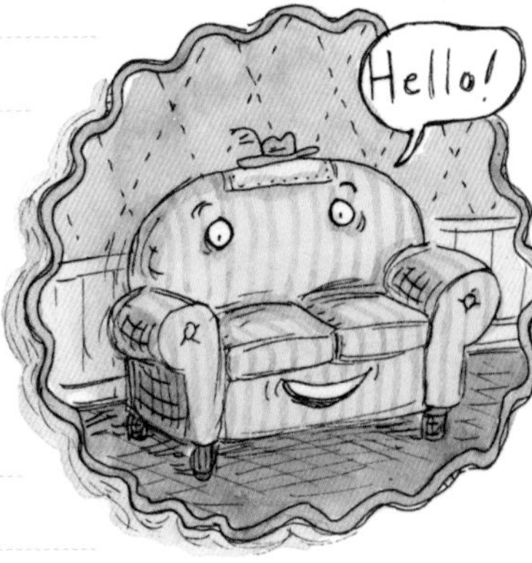
Hello!

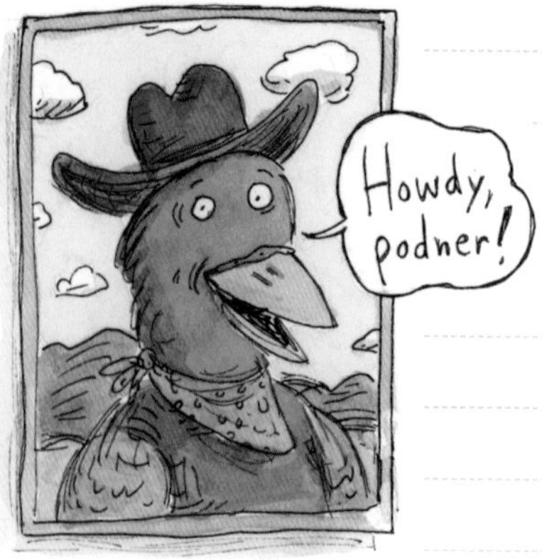
Howdy, podner!

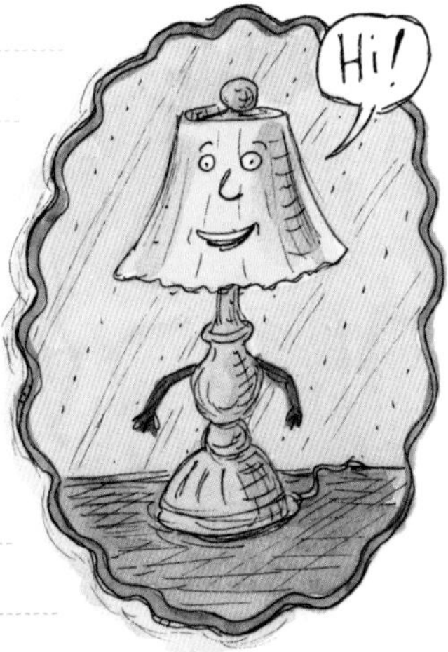
Hi!

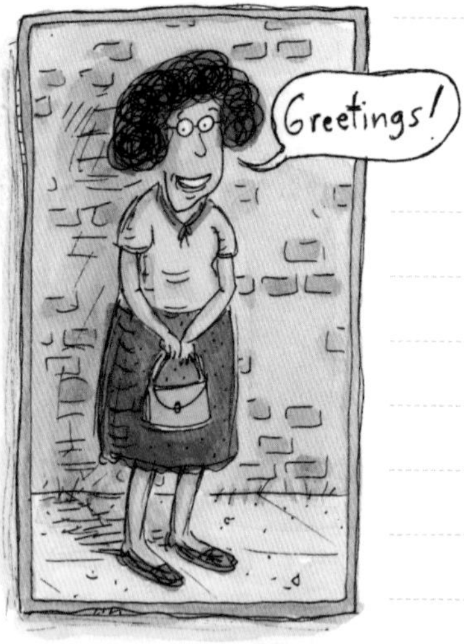
Greetings!

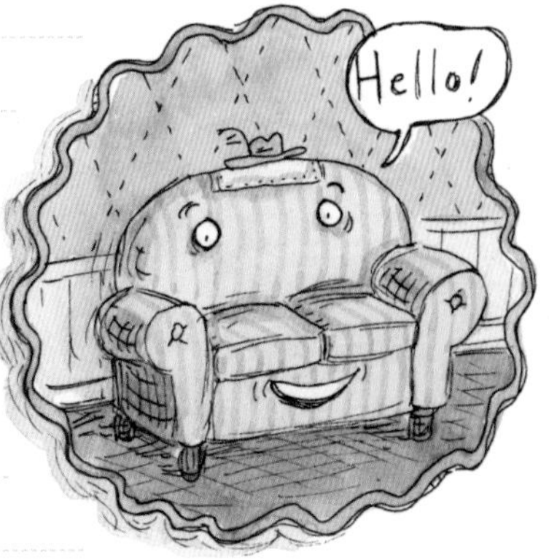
Hello!

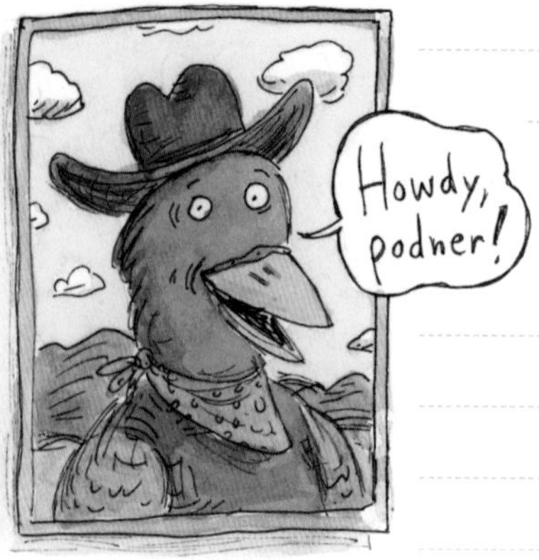
Howdy, podner!

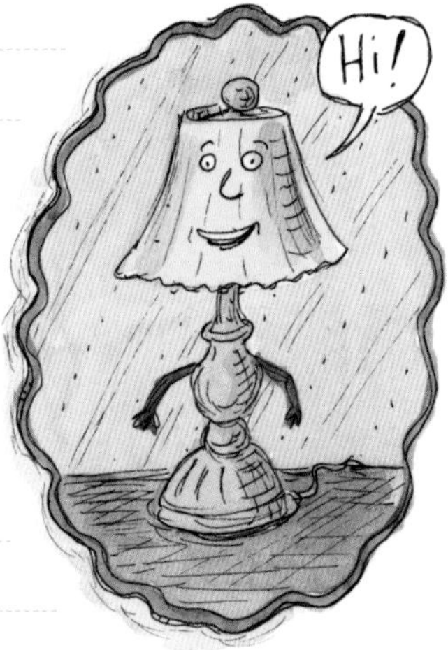
Hi!

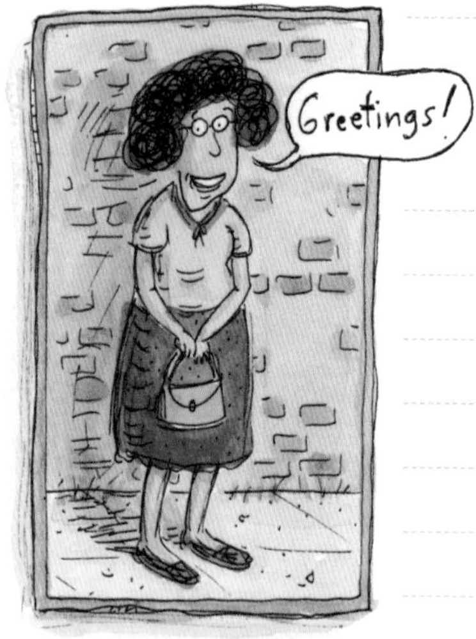
Greetings!

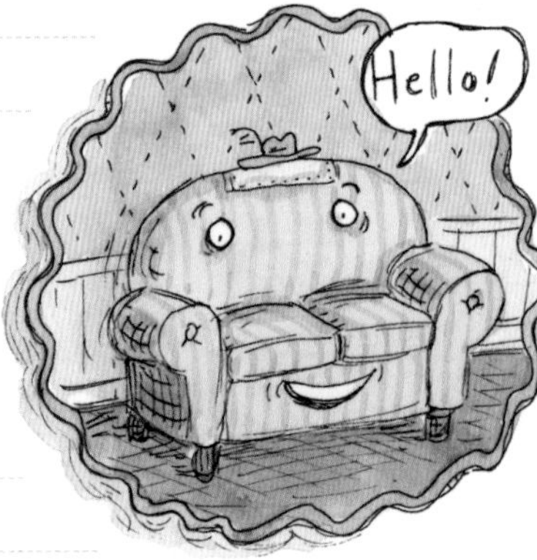
Hello!

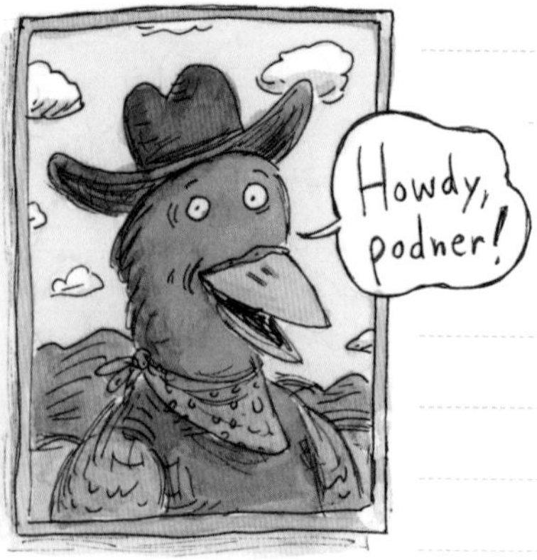
Howdy, podner!

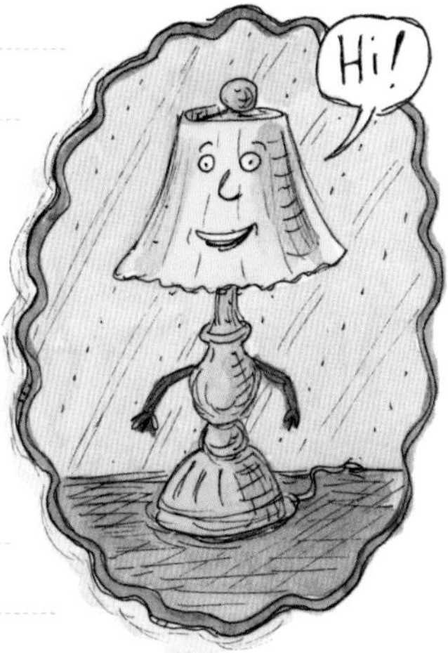
Hi!

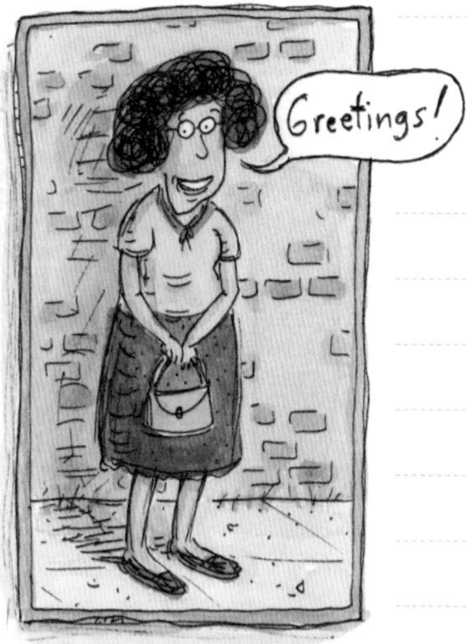
Greetings!

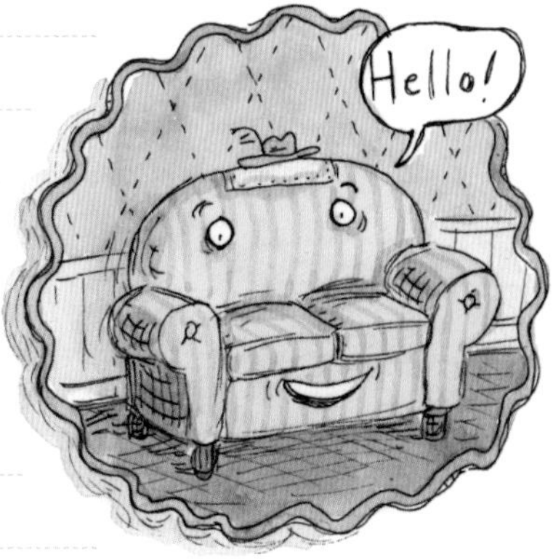
Hello!

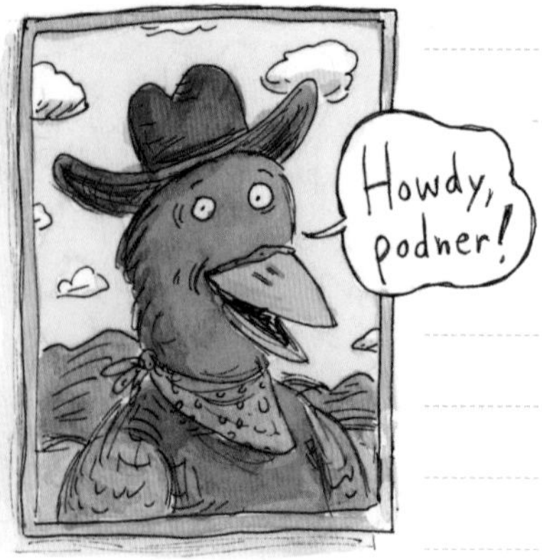
Howdy, podner!

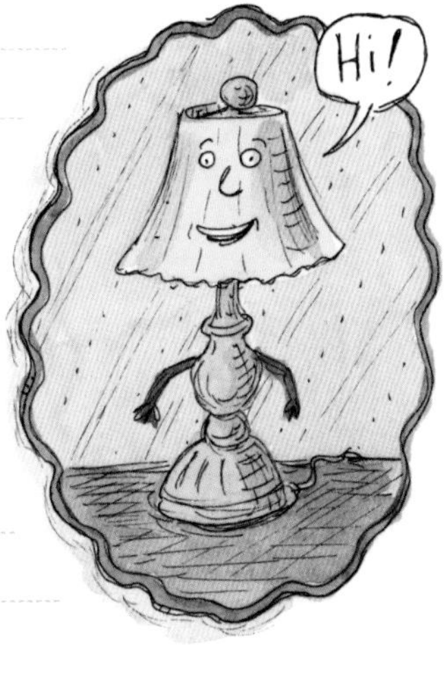
Hi!

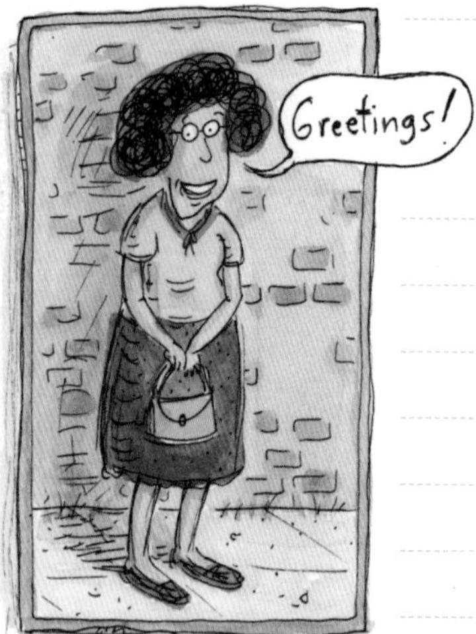
Greetings!

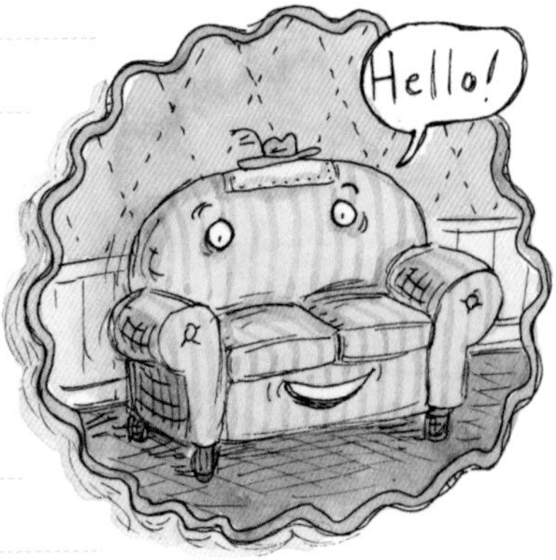
Hello!

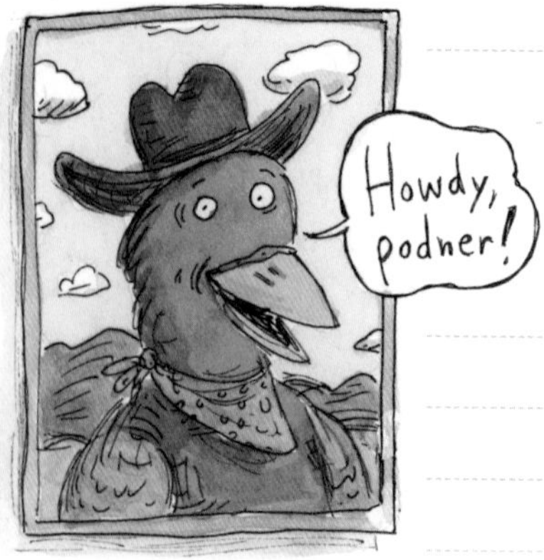
Howdy, podner!

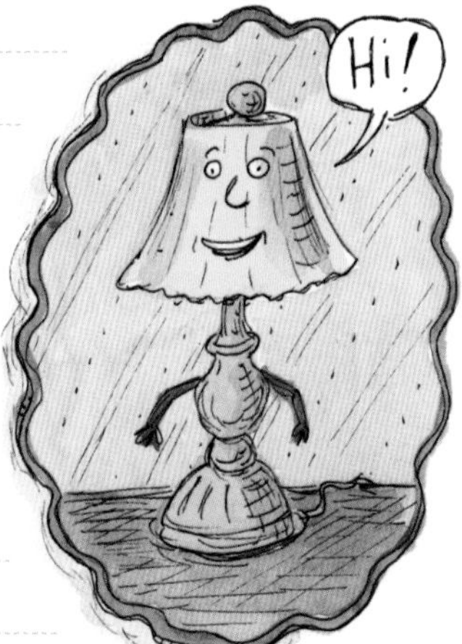
Hi!

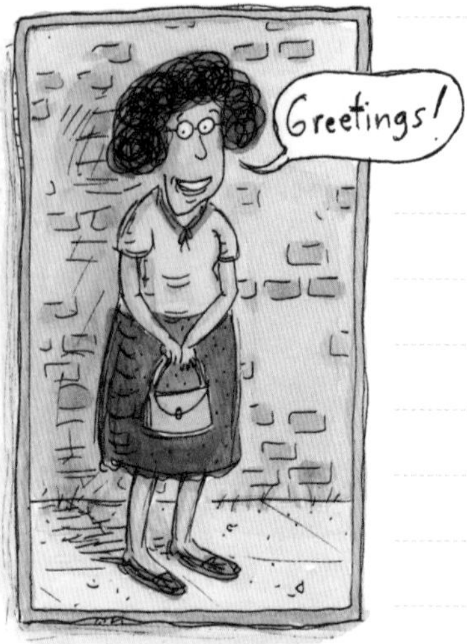
Greetings!

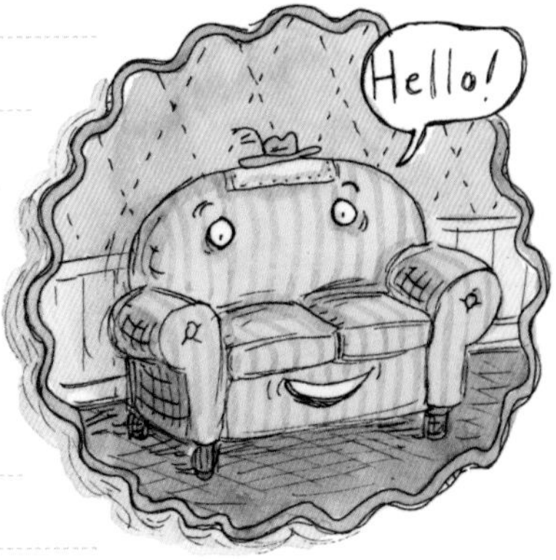
Hello!

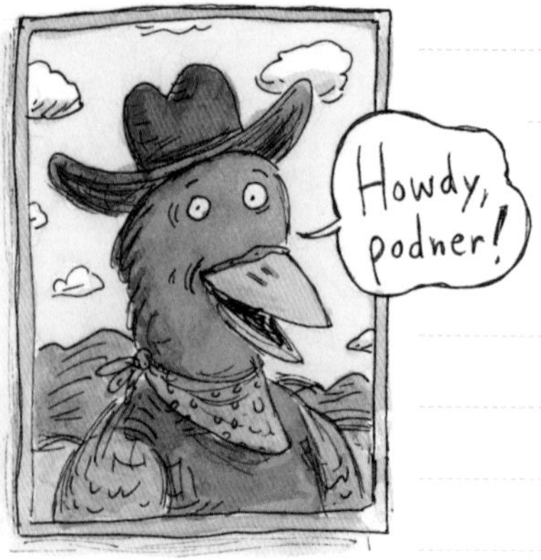
Howdy, podner!

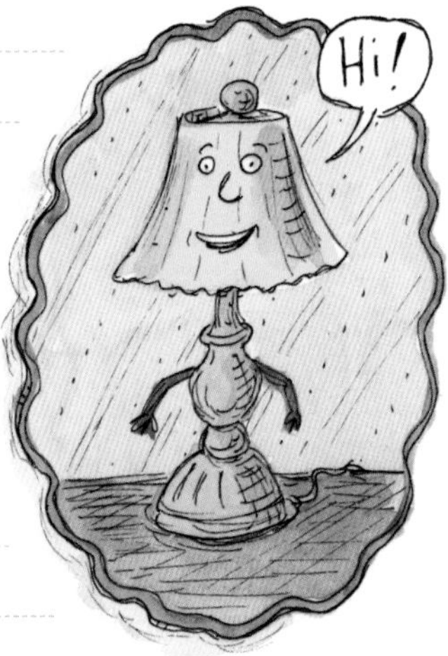
Hi!

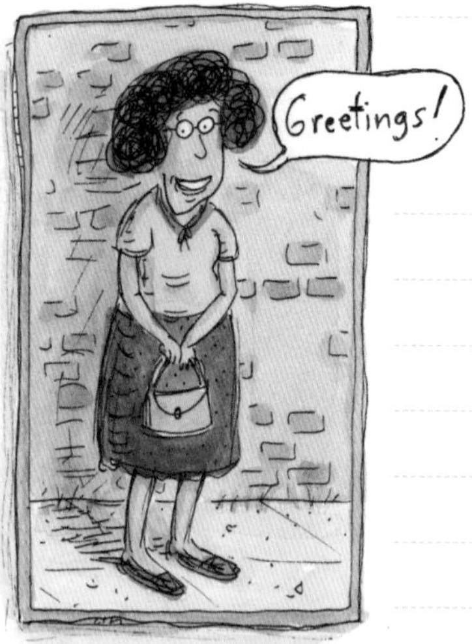
Greetings!

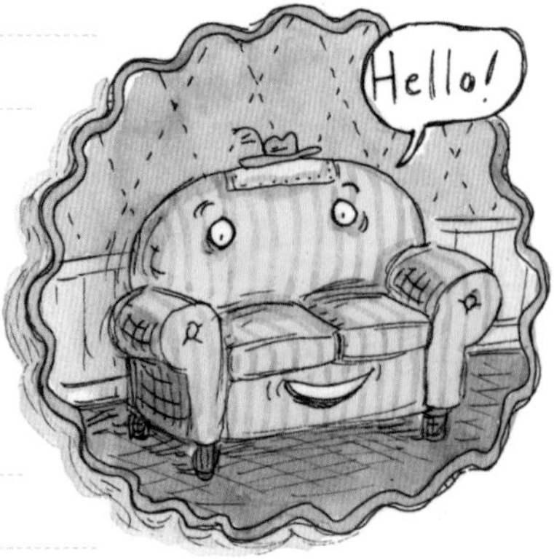
Hello!

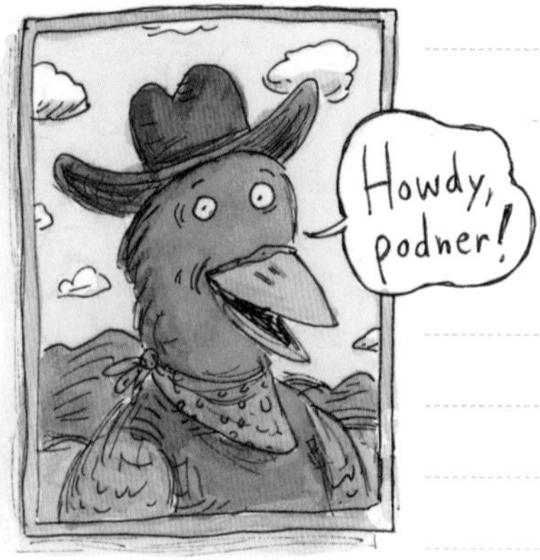
Howdy, podner!

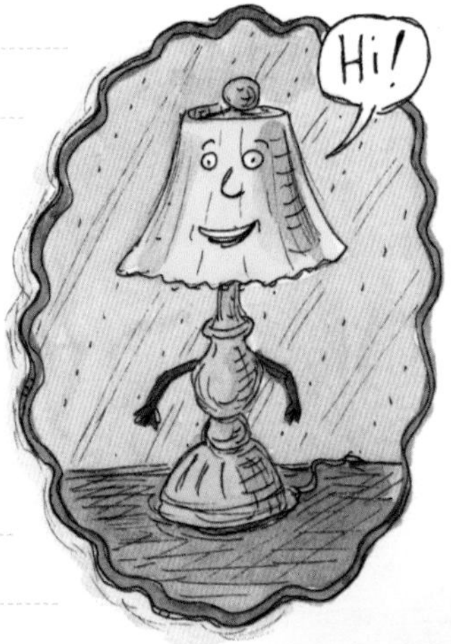
Hi!

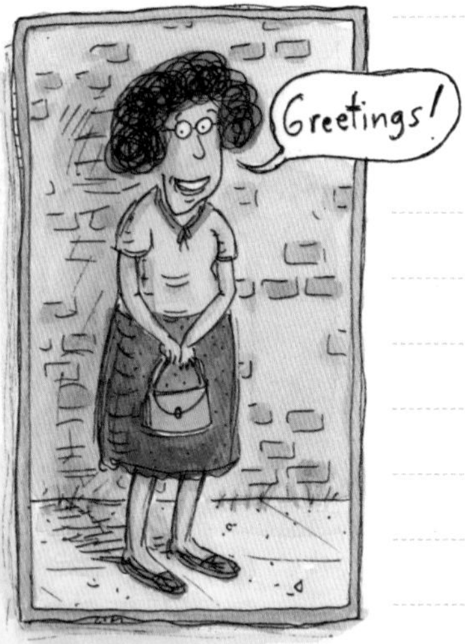
Greetings!